BIOGRAPHY OF RICHARD ROHR

TABLE OF CONTENTS

Introduction

Chapter 1

Chapter 2

Chapter 3

Chapter 4

Chapter 5

Conclusion

INTRODUCTION

One of the most significant spiritual thinkers of the modern period is Richard Rohr, a Franciscan writer and priest whose ideas have revolutionized Christian philosophy. Rohr has been delving deeply into faith, mysticism, and the changing role of the Church for almost 50 years, challenging traditional theological frameworks while staying firmly grounded in the Christian tradition. Millions of people around the world, including Catholics, Protestants, seekers, and skeptics, have found resonance in his writings because they offer a deep and sympathetic understanding of spirituality that relates to the challenges faced by contemporary Christians.

Rohr, who was born in Kansas in 1943, was drawn to the Franciscan way of life at a young age and embraced its focus on service, simplicity, and introspection. After being ordained in 1970, he immediately became well-known for his capacity to reconcile traditional religion with modern spiritual hunger. His teachings, which place a strong emphasis on what he refers to as "alternative orthodoxy," exhort followers of Christ to reject dogma and adopt a faith that is based on personal experience, introspection, and a profound understanding of God's presence in everything.

The impact of Rohr goes much beyond the pulpit. In Albuquerque, New Mexico, he founded the Center for Action and Contemplation (CAC), a group devoted to fusing social justice and spiritual practice. Many people have read and debated his publications, such as

"Falling Upward", "The Universal Christ", and "Everything Belongs", which have influenced the conversation about Christian spirituality in the twenty-first century. His prominence in interfaith and ecumenical groups, together with media appearances such as interviews with Brené Brown and Oprah Winfrey, have helped to elevate his voice.

However, Rohr has encountered some opposition along the way. Conservative Christian circles have criticized him for deviating too much from orthodoxy in his beliefs about inclusivity, scripture, and the nature of salvation. However, his ideas have been accepted in unexpected areas, even within the Catholic Church. Rohr's position within the larger Christian tradition was confirmed in 2022 when Pope Francis met with him one-on-one and urged him to carry on his teachings.

Rohr has struggled with heart illness and cancer, among other personal issues, in recent years. He declared in 2022 that he would be leaving public ministry because to health issues. His impact hasn't faded in spite of this. Discussions concerning faith, identity, and the place of the Church in a society that is changing quickly are still influenced by his ideas.

CHAPTER 1

The Path to Ministry and Faith

Born in 1943 in the small-town rhythms of Kansas, Richard Rohr's spiritual path started in the American heartland. Growing up in a pious Catholic family, Rohr was captivated by the customs, secrets, and rituals of religion from a young age. He was enthralled by the transformational power of religion, in contrast to those who inherit it as a simple cultural legacy. As he struggled with the conflict between the Church's formal theology and his natural feeling of a more expansive, experiential relationship with the divine, these formative years laid the groundwork for his lifelong pursuit of a deeper spiritual knowledge.

Rohr sensed a strong pull to religious life by the age of 18. He became a member of the Franciscan Order of Friars Minor (OFM) in 1961, which is renowned for its dedication to service, simplicity, and humility. He found great resonance in the Franciscans' emphasis on a different, justice-centered spirituality that valued experience over dogmatic doctrine and love over the rule of law. This was a precursor to the theological position he would eventually defend: a spirituality that aims to revitalize and broaden religious tradition rather than reject it.

Rohr received his theological education at the University of Dayton, where he graduated in 1970 with a Master of Theology. The Catholic Church underwent significant transformation during this time. A new period of openness was brought about by the Second Vatican

Council (1962–1965), which emphasized the role of the laity in the Church and promoted communication with people of different religions. Rohr was able to think about faith in a way that was both grounded in tradition and actively involved with the contemporary world because to the reforms of Vatican II.

In the same year, Rohr received his priestly ordination at the age of 27. He began his ministry in Cincinnati, Ohio, where he immediately gained recognition for his impassioned sermons and his capacity to engage young people who had grown weary of traditional religion. He established the New Jerusalem Community in 1971 after realizing the need for a more genuine and active spirituality. This deliberate community was an attempt to apply the principles of early Christianity to modern life. It was based on prayer, service, and communal living. Devout Catholics and seekers alike were drawn to the community because of its emphasis on social justice and personal growth.

However, the New Jerusalem Community had difficulties in spite of its early success. Rohr eventually became disillusioned with some elements of intentional community life, especially the propensity of idealistic organizations to become inflexible or isolated. He was still dedicated to encouraging genuine spiritual involvement, but he came to the realization that no one community could provide the profound renewal he was looking for. He took on a more global ministry that would impact lives all around the world since his vision went beyond

Cincinnati.

In Albuquerque, New Mexico, Rohr established the Center for Action and Contemplation (CAC) in 1986. CAC was intended to serve as a center for social activism, education, and spiritual development, in contrast to the New Jerusalem Community, which was centered on communal life. Rohr had a clear idea: activity and faith shouldn't be separated. Engagement with the world must logically follow contemplation, the profound, spiritual discipline of perceiving God. His teachings were based on this conviction, which contradicted the idea that faith was only about one's own salvation. Rather, he advocated for a spirituality that was deeply involved in healing, inclusivity, and justice.

The Living School for activity and Contemplation, which Rohr founded through CAC, has since taught thousands of people a spiritual method that combines mystical awareness with practical activity in the world. Seven topics that Rohr established over decades of study, meditation, and pastoral work form the foundation of the school's curriculum. His book "Yes, And..." outlines these concepts, which inspire students to embrace paradox, transcend binary thinking, and see the divine in everything.

Rohr's audience grew along with his ministry. His talks, retreats, and books started to reach people outside of the Catholic community. Evangelicals, Protestants, former Catholics, and even nonreligious people discovered a spirituality in his writings that spoke to their innermost concerns. He stands out as a teacher because of his capacity to transform difficult theological and mystical concepts into understandable, intensely personal insights.

Rohr never lost sight of his Franciscan heritage during his travels. Themes of simplicity, humility, and the holiness of all creation recur frequently in his teachings. Like St. Francis of Assisi, he aimed to reveal the fundamental truth of religion—that God is love and that love is the energy that creates and maintains the universe—by removing its superfluous accoutrements.

Reinforcing institutional power was never the goal of Rohr's journey into faith and service. Rather, it aimed to reawaken the Church and everyone who pursued truth to a more inclusive, expansive, and profoundly transformational spirituality. His life's work has been an appeal to recover the contemplative core of Christianity, to accept mystery instead of certainty, and to view faith as a dynamic, ever-evolving relationship with God rather than a collection of dogmatic doctrines.

His influence hasn't waned even after he retired from active ministry in 2022 due to health issues. His continuing vision is demonstrated by the communities he established, the books he authored, and the many lives he impacted. Richard Rohr's journey from a young Kansas friar to a globally recognized spiritual teacher has been one of constant growth—an invitation to everyone who comes into contact with his work to transcend their own boundaries and enter the immense, endless wonder of God.

CHAPTER 2

Accepting the Mystical Route

Richard Rohr was already well-known as a powerful spiritual teacher by the time he was in the middle of his career. However, he intensified his attention on Christian mysticism during this time, which is an old but frequently disregarded Church tradition. According to Rohr, the core of faith was in direct, experienced unity with the Divine, even though a large portion of contemporary Christianity had become focused on doctrine, regulations, and moralistic issues. A desire to recover this mystical wisdom—a spirituality founded on a close connection with the divine rather than strict belief systems—became more and more evident in his teachings.

According to Rohr, mysticism has nothing to do with mystical understanding or unearthly experiences. It was about recognizing truth for what it is: God's presence permeates every second, every individual, and every aspect of creation. He frequently cited Jesus as the pinnacle of mysticism, someone who profoundly embodied spiritual unity rather than just teaching about it. Rohr saw Jesus' radical teachings on forgiveness, love, and non-dual consciousness as an invitation for everyone to follow the same path, not just something to be praised.

The eternal wisdom tradition, which holds that all great religious traditions have a fundamental truth, had a significant impact on Rohr's investigation of mysticism. He was deeply anchored in

Christianity, but he frequently borrowed ideas from other religions, such as Buddhism, Sufism, and meditative Judaism. In addition to the insights of earlier individuals like Meister Eckhart, Julian of Norwich, and the Desert Fathers and Mothers, he was especially influenced by the works of mystics from the 20th century, such as Thomas Merton and Evelyn Underhill. Drawing from these sources, Rohr constructed a concept of spirituality that aimed to dismantle rather than erect boundaries, and that was expansive rather than restrictive.

Rohr's focus on non-dual thinking has been one of his most significant contributions to contemporary spirituality. He has frequently bemoaned the "either/or" mentality that has gripped Western Christianity, categorizing people as either saved or unsaved, good or terrible, or insiders or outsiders. Mysticism, on the other hand, welcomes paradox. It permits uncertainty, intricacy, and enigma. Rohr has emphasized time and again that the spiritual path is about learning to live in the midst of doubt with faith and openness, not about achieving complete assurance.

The concept of the "True Self" and the "False Self," which has its roots in Christian mysticism but is also influenced by psychological theories, especially Carl Jung's, is a central theme in his writings. According to Rohr, the False Self is the identity we create for ourselves based on approval from others—our ego-driven need to succeed, win admiration, and fit in with society's expectations. We put it on to feel secure and significant in the world. The True Self, the aspect of ourselves that is already united with God, is located beneath this False Self. According to Rohr, the goal of the spiritual journey is to find who we already are rather than to change into someone new.

This issue is thoroughly examined in his book "Immortal Diamond: The Search for Our True Self", which makes the case that a large portion of contemporary Christianity has placed too much emphasis on personal morality and sin control at the expense of the deep inner transformation that Jesus truly advocated. According to Rohr, the resurrection is a metaphor for this metamorphosis—a shift from the tiny, ego-driven self to the enormous, divine self that has always existed within of us—rather than merely a historical occurrence.

Contemplative meditation is one of the methods Rohr assists individuals in reaching this higher state of consciousness. He has been a fervent supporter of Christian meditation and centering prayer throughout his career, practices that enable people to calm their minds and have direct encounters with God. Contemplative prayer encourages a surrender of control, a readiness to rest in God's presence without trying to understand or define it, in contrast to petitionary prayer, which frequently serves to strengthen the ego's goals and concerns. Contemplation is a "long, loving look at the real," according to Rohr, a practice that enables one to see with the soul's eyes rather than just the mind's.

He has questioned several of

the tenets of contemporary institutional Christianity as a result of his emphasis on introspection. He contends that an excessive amount of religious practice has been centered on external authority—attending services, abiding by doctrine, and following rules—instead than assisting individuals in cultivating their own inner lives with God. Although he acknowledges the importance of tradition, he feels that religion can become legalistic and lifeless in the absence of firsthand encounters with the Divine. He contends that this is among the causes of the widespread disengagement from organized religion among individuals, particularly among younger generations. They are looking for a close contact with the sacred, something more profound than institutional affiliation.

There has been some dispute around Rohr's involvement with mysticism. He is accused by some conservative theologians of deviating too much from conventional Christian teaching because of his emphasis on interior experience, which they claim could result in subjective interpretations.

CHAPTER 3

The Path to Reflection

As Richard Rohr's spiritual development progressed, he came to view contemplation as a radical and essential method of interacting with the world, rather than as a passive or esoteric activity. For Rohr, contemplation was about seeing life more clearly, through the eyes of divine love, rather than retreating from it. It was a route for anyone looking for a more genuine, awakened life, not simply mystics or monks.

Both his Franciscan heritage and his experiences with many wisdom traditions influenced his dedication to introspection. For a long time, the Franciscan Order has placed a strong emphasis on prayer, nature, and a direct, unmediated communion with God. Nonetheless, Rohr also drew heavily from other Christian contemplatives, like the anonymous author of "The Cloud of Unknowing", a medieval work that teaches letting go of thoughts in order to rest in divine presence, and Thomas Merton, who taught him about centering prayer.

According to Rohr, contemplation was about going beyond thought entirely—into what he frequently referred to as a "long, loving look at the real"—rather than about thinking more about God. His teachings underwent a sea change when he moved from intellectualizing religion to directly experiencing it. He started to stress that genuine spirituality was about transformation—about being more conscious, more present, and more intimately linked to God and other people—rather than ideas or changing one's conduct.

One of Rohr's most important discoveries was that contemplation enables one to transcend what he referred to as the "dualistic mind." He maintained that the "either/or" mentality that pits good against evil, right against wrong, saved against lost, has ensnared Western Christianity. He felt that this dualistic attitude resulted in divisiveness, judgment, and a lack of empathy. The heart is opened to paradox, mystery, and the capacity to keep contradictions in tension without having to resolve them via reflection, on the other hand. True wisdom, according to Rohr, arises in this area.

His focus on contemplation was not merely theoretical; it had real-world applications for everything from social justice to individual spiritual development. He thought that activism and moral outrage might quickly turn into reactive, violent, or ego-driven behavior if they had a meditative basis. Conversely, contemplation produced the inner calm required for persistent, caring action. Rohr frequently cited Jesus' forty days in the desert as an illustration of reflection followed by action. Jesus withdrew into quiet before to starting his public ministry, serving as a metaphor for how profound inner work comes before significant external work.

Centering prayer, which he advocated as a means for contemporary seekers to encounter God beyond words, was at the core of his contemplative teaching. Centering prayer, which has its roots in the Christian mystical tradition, is letting go of thoughts rather than interacting with them and silently accepting God's presence. According to Rohr, this practice is a kind of surrender and a counterbalance to the ego's incessant demand for certainty, control, and explanation. He frequently urged people to spend twenty minutes a day sitting in quiet, not to "achieve" anything but to learn to be at ease just by being in God's presence.

His contemplative teachings were not limited to the Christian faith however. Interfaith discussion had a significant impact on Rohr, who believed that Christian mysticism was compatible with the contemplative practices of Buddhism, Sufism, and indigenous spirituality. He frequently emphasized how Jesus himself embraced the interconnectedness of all things and lived in a non-dual state of awareness. Rohr felt that all true spiritual traditions led to the same universal truths and did not view other religions as rivals.

Institutional Christianity did not always embrace Rohr's focus on introspection. While some detractors feared that his interfaith friendliness obscured crucial theological distinctions, others charged that he had deviated too much from conventional orthodoxy. However, Rohr stuck to his conviction that genuine Christianity required introspection. He saw it as a means of experiencing the deeper meaning of doctrine rather than as a rejection of it.

Rohr proceeded to spread this vision by welcoming individuals into a spirituality that was founded on personal experience rather than strict doctrine through his books, retreats, and the Center for Action and Contemplation. Many people found resonance in his message, especially those who had felt excluded by traditional religion. Many found that Rohr's teachings provided a means of reclaiming their faith—not as a collection of laws but rather as a close, continuous relationship with God.

In addition to being a theological exercise, his journey into contemplation was intensely personal. Rohr frequently talked about how his own practice had taught him to let go of the urge to control results, defend his name, or be correct. He was softer, more patient, and more forgiving—not only of other people, but also of himself—after reflecting. He felt that the capacity to navigate the world with an open heart was the real reward of living a thoughtful life.

CHAPTER 4

The Development of a Contemplative Vision

Although Richard Rohr was already well-known as a Catholic Church thinker by the 1980s, it was in this decade that his distinctive vision for spiritual development started to take shape in a more tangible and long-lasting manner. His conviction that Christianity required a more profound, introspective approach—one that was not limited to strict doctrine but rather rooted in a direct, lived experience of

God—was cemented by his early experiences as a Franciscan priest, as well as his involvement with social justice, psychology, and interfaith discussion. This belief would eventually drive him to establish the Center for Action and Contemplation (CAC), one of the most significant spiritual organizations of the modern period.

Although Rohr had found great fulfillment in his work with Cincinnati's New Jerusalem Community, he realized that something was lacking. Although the community was flourishing, he felt compelled to establish a place where those who were seeking spirituality could interact with Christianity in a way that combined introspection with purposeful activity. He had grown to feel that the conventional approach of religious formation frequently prioritized right belief, or orthodoxy, over appropriate behavior, or orthopraxy. He aimed to develop a way that integrated the two, encouraging people to comprehend theological ideas and live them out in their everyday lives.

Rohr's move to Albuquerque, New Mexico, in 1986 would turn out to be crucial to his spiritual development. With its vast deserts, majestic mountains, and profound indigenous spiritual origins, the American Southwest offered the perfect backdrop for his goals. In this setting, he envisioned a space where individuals from diverse backgrounds—priests, laypeople, activists, and seekers—could delve into a faith that was profoundly personal yet universal. The CAC, an organization that would later serve as a pillar of contemporary contemplative Christianity, was founded in this environment.

From the beginning, the CAC's goal was crystal clear: to provide a bridge between thought and action. According to Rohr, a lot of religious organizations have either pushed too much toward activity, missing the depth that spiritual practice could offer, or too much toward contemplation, encouraging introspection at the expense of social interaction. Harmonizing these two components was his aim. He frequently referred to contemplation as a type of deep seeing, or the capacity to view the world not through division and judgment but through the eyes of love and union. Therefore, the logical result of such seeing was action. People would naturally be drawn to justice, compassion, and service as they developed a knowledge of God's presence in everything.

The idea of the "True Self" and the "False Self," which Rohr would further develop during his career, lay at the core of his reflective worldview. According to his theory, a large portion of human misery results from an excessive identification with the False Self, which is our ego-driven identity that is influenced by fears, societal expectations, and delusions of separateness. Contrarily, the True Self was each person's deeper, divinely endowed essence. Rohr's teachings inspired people to awaken to a bigger, more interconnected reality and transcend their constrained self-perceptions.

Spiritual searchers from many denominations and even religions found great resonance in this idea. As the CAC expanded, it started providing seminars, retreats, and eventually online courses with the goal of helping people go through this process of self-transformation. Rohr's method was distinct because it blended ideas from psychology, Eastern philosophy, and contemporary science with aspects of traditional Christian mysticism. Since truth was not the sole purview of any one tradition, he was not hesitant to draw from a variety of sources.

Rohr's voice started to be

heard by more people as the CAC rose to popularity. The foundation for his later, more expansive works was established by his early works, such as "Everything Belongs" and "The Naked Now". Those who wanted to better understand their own spiritual composition were especially interested in his lessons on the Enneagram, a spiritual personality system with ancient Christian roots. Rohr was a popular speaker and author because of his ability to simplify difficult theological concepts into understandable, useful insight.

Rohr had solidified his position as one of the most influential figures in modern Christian spirituality by the end of the 1990s. The CAC had developed into a gathering place for people who were looking for a more radical, inclusive religion that respected both the need for progress and the wisdom of tradition. In addition to being theoretical, Rohr's contemplative vision was an invitation to a lived experience of divine love—a path that necessitated both engagement and surrender, stillness and activity.

This period in Rohr's life marked a sea change and prepared the ground for his subsequent body of work. His role as a global spiritual teacher would soon be even more completely realized, with the CAC thriving and his teachings reaching an ever-increasing audience. However, he stayed true to the Franciscan principles of service, simplicity, and humility despite his growing power. The goal of Rohr's contemplative approach was to awaken people's hearts and minds to the truth of God's presence in everything, not to acknowledge oneself. And he was just getting started on this.

CHAPTER 5

A Voice for a Changing Religious Environment

Richard Rohr's impact has expanded much beyond the contemplative circles where he first became well-known by the turn of the twenty-first century. He had previously created a life-changing environment for spiritual searchers as the founder of the Center for Action and Contemplation (CAC) in Albuquerque. However, the needs of people looking for faith that could endure the difficulties of contemporary life were evolving along with the world around him. For Rohr and Christianity in general, the early 2000s were a time of significant change. Many Christians were challenging established faith structures as a result of postmodernism's growth, growing disenchantment with institutional religion, and changing societal values. During this period, Rohr's voice emerged as one of the most persuasive manuals for those negotiating the ambiguities of faith.

According to Rohr, a lot of individuals were leaving

traditional religious organizations not because they were no longer interested in spirituality but rather because they were looking for something more profound that would allow them to reconcile their faith with their everyday lives. He frequently discussed how strict, dogmatic Christian doctrines were ignoring the complexity of the human experience. Instead of rejecting tradition, he responded by proposing a broader, more inclusive, and more reflective interpretation of it.

The idea of "nondual consciousness"—the notion that a large portion of human suffering results from a binary way of thinking that splits the world into opposites—good and terrible, saved and unsaved, right and wrong—was at the heart of Rohr's developing message. Spiritual growth, in his opinion, entailed overcoming this dualistic perspective and achieving a more comprehensive, cohesive consciousness. He urged people to feel the divine presence in everything rather than viewing God as distinct from creation. This concept, which has its roots in Christian mysticism, struck a chord with a generation of seekers who were drawn to contemplative practice and interspiritual discussion.

Meanwhile, Rohr's message was still being shaped by his teachings on the "True Self and False Self". He maintained that rather than helping individuals change on the inside, a large portion of contemporary Christianity had become fixated on outward behavior, such as following the law or fitting in with institutional standards. According to him, the True

Self is the most profound identity that each individual possesses; it is the divine imprint that transcends ego and societal conditioning. On the other hand, the False Self was the transient identity formed by pride, anxiety, and a need for approval from others. As the core of Christian redemption, Rohr's teaching became an invitation to let go of the False Self and live into the freedom of the True Self.

Rohr also started to actively participate in "emerging theological discussions" that questioned conventional ideas of faith around this time. One of his most important contributions to modern Christian philosophy was his investigation of the "Universal Christ". Rohr highlighted Christ as a cosmic reality—the everlasting presence of God embedded in all of creation—as opposed to a limited view of Christ as being the historical person of Jesus. Despite having its roots in early Christian theology, this concept seemed radical to people used to a more constrained understanding of Christ's function. However, Rohr maintained that this constituted a return to the mystical underpinnings of Christian orthodoxy rather than a break from it.

Those struggling with faith reconstruction and deconstruction were drawn to his expanding body of work, which included books like 'The Naked Now' and 'Falling Upward'. He addressed those who longed for a purposeful spiritual life but felt alienated by strict church systems. Those who had been harmed by religion—whether by moral dogmatism, exclusionary theology, or church scandals—were particularly affected by his message. Instead of stifling their inquiries, Rohr's teachings provided them with an alternative path ahead.

During this period, Rohr's leadership at the CAC grew in addition to his writing and teaching. Attracting seekers from various backgrounds—Catholics, Protestants, and even people outside of conventional Christian frameworks—the institute developed into a center for spiritual formation. An intense, immersive experience in contemplative wisdom was offered by programs like the Living School for Action and Contemplation, which Rohr co-founded. Along with Christian mystics like Teresa of Ávila and St. John of the Cross, students also studied Buddhism, Sufism, and indigenous customs. Not everyone agreed with Rohr's inclusive stance; some detractors claimed he was endorsing syncretism or weakening Christianity. Rohr, however, was unfazed because he thought that truth was not limited to any one tradition.

This period of Rohr's life was

also marked by his growing interest in "social justice issues". Although he had always highlighted the link between reflection and action, he became much more outspoken in the 2000s against topics like environmental degradation, economic inequality, and racial injustice. Rohr viewed these issues as profoundly spiritual rather than political. He maintained that reflection ought to result in a deeper understanding of suffering and, eventually, a dedication to justice. His views, which advocated for structural change as opposed to just charitable giving, were consistent with Christianity's prophetic history.

Rohr's impact grew even more as he moved into his older years. He had developed into a spiritual teacher with a global following, not merely a Franciscan priest addressing small groups of contemplative people. People of many ages, denominations, and even religious affiliations were able to benefit from his insight. Rohr, however, stayed true to the simplicity and humility that had always characterized his Franciscan vocation in spite of his rising celebrity. He frequently reminded his followers that the purpose of spirituality was to let go and submit to divine love, not to gain prestige or knowledge.

Rohr changed from being a contemplative leader to a spiritual elder during this time in his life. After decades of establishing a new approach to faith, he suddenly observed a world that was becoming more and more prepared for the wisdom he had been providing. The twenty-first century was turning out to be a turbulent but also exciting time, one in which spirituality could become a transformational force if it were treated with courage and openness. And throughout this developing narrative, Rohr's voice continued to be a beacon of hope, urging listeners to pursue the greater mystery of God rather than certainty.

CONCLUSION

A Tradition of Knowledge and Change

Even as Richard Rohr's life and career came to an end, his impact on modern spirituality was already irrevocable. He was now more than just a Franciscan priest; he was a mentor to people who were trying to balance their faith with the demands of contemporary life. In addition to assisting people in strengthening their spiritual practices, his teachings helped rethink Christianity in general. Rohr had spent decades encouraging people to transcend dogmatic ideologies and enter a lived experience of divine love, all the while maintaining an unshakeable dedication to contemplative wisdom, inclusivity, and social justice.

Rohr's ability to explain the spiritual path in a way that appealed to seekers from a variety of backgrounds was fundamental to his influence. For individuals who felt limited by conventional religious frameworks, his understanding of "nondual consciousness", the "True

Self and False Self", and the "Universal Christ" offered a framework. He had a unique talent for bringing mystical ideas down to earth, guiding people through the conflicts between certainty and mystery, faith and doubt, and exile and belonging. By doing this, he provided not only religious concepts but also a road toward change, one that inspired people to accept life's beauty and pain as a necessary component of their spiritual development.

Rohr's ability to address the spiritual disillusionment that had become so pervasive in the modern society was one of his most significant accomplishments. Many of his supporters had become disillusioned with the institutional church due to its power struggles, restrictive policies, and unwillingness to adapt. Rohr acknowledged their difficulties and guided them toward a more profound and expansive faith, but he did not expect them to ignore these disappointments. He reminded them that love, not laws, was the central message of Christianity. It's about inclusion, not exclusion. It's about surrender, not control.

Even as his own spiritual path changed, Rohr stayed steadfastly committed to his purpose in his senior years, teaching, writing, and mentoring. He realized that wisdom, like life itself, required a constant readiness to unlearn, adapt, and let go; that spiritual growth was never static. This insight was evident in his thoughts on aging, pain, and death, as he openly discussed the process of letting go of what he referred to as the "second half of life." True knowledge, according to Rohr's long-standing teachings, comes from accepting the uncertainty rather than holding onto certainties. He exemplified this lesson as he grew older, showing how the road of introspection eventually results in a deep faith in divine mystery.

However, his impact went well beyond individual spirituality. Additionally, Rohr had influenced the 21st-century discourse about faith in general. Innumerable people looking for a more purposeful way to interact with the world have continued to get spiritual formation from his work at the "Center for Action and

Contemplation (CAC)". A new generation of activists, pastors, and laypeople who regarded social justice as a logical progression of genuine spirituality rather than a political position were inspired by his focus on the link between contemplation and action. Rohr frequently reminded his followers that introspection alone was insufficient and that the path must constantly lead outward, toward greater service and compassion.

Even though Rohr received a lot of praise, he never tried to start a movement. By always pointing beyond himself to the larger truths he aimed to communicate, he resisted the lure of spiritual stardom. He used to joke that he had failed in his aim if people could recall his name but not the message. One of his most remarkable traits was probably his humility, which was a reflection of his Franciscan lifelong dedication to simplicity, service, and surrender.

Rohr's legacy became evident as his time on the spiritual stage dwindled: he had contributed to the recovery of Christianity's mystical core for a new age. He had reminded everyone that faith is about living into the mystery of divine love, not about demonstrating one's convictions. He demonstrated that developing the ability to hold questions with grace rather than having all the answers is a sign of spiritual maturity. Above all, he had lived out the same teaching he taught: that God is not far away but rather is present in everything; that divine love is not something we have to earn but has always existed.

Long after he had delivered his final sermon, his presence,

words, and wisdom would still influence the spiritual landscape. In addition to changing lives, Richard Rohr altered people's perceptions of what it meant to be completely alive. And in doing so, his work would live on, reverberating in the hearts of those who had been influenced by his teachings and pointing the way for future generations toward a more profound and caring perspective on the world.